Plant Style

Designed by Ngaio Parr

Edited by Lorna Hendry

Styled by Alana Langan

Plant Style copyright © 2017 Thames & Hudson
Text copyright © 2017 Alana Langan and Jacqui Vidal
Photographs copyright © 2017 Annette O'Brien

First published in 2018 in hardcover in the United States of America by Thames & Hudson Inc., 500 Fifth Avenue, New York, New York 10110

thamesandhudsonusa.com

Library of Congress Catalog Card Number: 2018931554

ISBN 978-0-500-50103-0

Printed and bound in China by 1010 Ltd.

Plant Style

How to greenify your space

—

Alana Langan & Jacqui Vidal
of *Ivy Muse*

Photography by Annette O'Brien

CONTENTS

01

—

Introduction

Jacqui Vidal and Alana Langan

There's a special feeling you get when you walk into a room filled with thriving greenery, and it usually results in a smile. That's why plants are a stylist's best friend. Although there's a bit more to consider when styling your home with plants than with inanimate objects, the rewards are well worth it. Plants add softness, warmth and remind us of nature, which makes us happy. They enliven our homes and create a sanctuary for us to retreat to after a long day, but the real secret lies in their ability to transform an interior into something magical.

We launched Ivy Muse, our botanical wares studio, in 2014 with a goal to encourage creativity with greenery. Two long-time friends – one interior stylist and one gallerist – we shared a passion for design and plants. Although we were both already plant lovers, our appreciation for all things botanical has grown stronger every day. We design with longevity in mind, making sure our pieces can be used in a variety of ways and adapted for use over time. We love our jobs. Working with plants is an inspiring and rewarding pursuit. We're also part of a passionate community and a growing tribe of houseplant collectors.

Every day, our customers tell us that they want to create a plant-filled sanctuary at home but don't know where to start. This book is the answer. From the basics, like which plants go where and what tools you will need, to deconstructing the task of creating a stunning green shelfie, we share our knowledge of styling with plants. We show you how to make a perfect green-themed tablescape and create a jungle-like boudoir, and offer

practical advice about how to add plants to bathrooms, kitchens and every room in between.

The plants in this book are our favourites. Most of them can be purchased from any local nursery or plant shop. We have chosen them for their ease of care, their hardy temperament and we've also included lots of options for beginners and more experienced plant collectors. Throughout the book we refer to plants by their common name, but we've also listed their Latin names in the plant index.

Maybe you're just at the start of your journey with plants and aren't sure where to begin. Perhaps you are already a plant fanatic with a burgeoning collection. You might be a city dweller in a pint-sized apartment, or you may call a five-bedroom weatherboard in the suburbs home. This book will help you select, arrange and style plants to greenify your home and make the most of the space you have, whatever that may be.

02

—

What is
plant styling?

Every space in your home, no matter what size,
is a unique opportunity to reflect who you are
and what you love. It's the small details that
make a home – a tiny personal touch here, a
much-loved object there – and plants, with all
their superstar qualities, can really shine.

Styling your home with plants isn't a new idea. The Egyptians were the first people to bring plants indoors as decorative items. Images of potted plants have been found in ancient tombs that date back thousands of years. In the fifteenth century, houseplants spread across Europe and exotic plants became objects of desire.

During the Victorian era, many of the typical houseplant varieties that we still grow today were brought to Europe from their native New World environments. However, it wasn't until the 1950s that indoor plants became commonplace, helped along by the increasing popularity of accessories like macramé hangers, plant stands and terrariums.

Houseplants were hugely popular in the 1970s – in fact, plants were the decorating detail that defined that period. You only need to flick through old magazines or do a little online research to see that in those days they certainly knew a thing or two about living with greenery.

Nowadays, as the trend towards minimal, contemporary homes becomes more common, so does the need to soften those spaces and reconnect with nature.

LIVING WITH PLANTS

Whether you're keen to turn your whole house into a jungle or are planning to add a touch of greenery here and there, keep in mind that plants are not purely ornamental. They are alive, they do grow, they can be messy and they are always changing – but this is exactly what makes them so beautiful.

There is a theory that humans are drawn to other living things, and we're inclined to agree. Caring for plants can be a rewarding and long-lasting endeavour that enriches your life. It offers time for solitude and quiet contemplation away from the hustle and bustle of everyday life.

It can also be a fun experience to share with the rest of the family. Children love to water plants and watch new leaves unfurl. Houseplants can also foster wider relationships. You can share ideas with friends, swap cuttings with neighbours or even join a botanical society.

Plants are also budget-friendly. The larger or more rare varieties can be a little more expensive, but there are always cheaper options. And long after you've given up chasing the latest trend in furniture or decor items, your plants will still be growing and bringing beauty into your home for many years to come.

They can also be beneficial to your health. Studies have shown that your green-leafed friends have a positive effect on your environment and wellbeing. They act as air filters, reducing household toxins, like the chemicals and glues used in carpets and furniture, as well as reducing stress and increasing creativity and productivity.

If you aren't convinced yet, here's the real kicker. Plants look damn pretty. A well-placed plant can have a huge impact on a set of shelves and a bold tree can liven up a dull corner in the blink of an eye. Whether it's a few pots on a windowsill or an entire room dedicated to your plant gang, indoor plants will enhance your home in many ways.

THE BASICS

Styling with plants is not a science. There's no single rule – other than keeping them alive, of course! Learn what works for you, understand the conditions of the spaces in your home and if something doesn't look right, move it. It's all about having fun and creating something beautiful. Like most things in life, with a little practice and know-how, you'll be styling your plants like a professional in no time. All you need is a few handy tips and tricks. Don't be afraid. Trust us.

PLAN

The first thing you need to do is get an idea of the look you want to achieve. Trawl websites. Check out Pinterest and Instagram. Flick through magazines, books or anything else that catches your eye. Once you figure out what kind of plants you love and the style you're going for, you can assess how suitable those varieties are for your space.

Identify the space you have to work with. Measure it so that you know what you're dealing with. If you find it hard to imagine how plants might look in the space, do a sketch. Consider the basic principles of interior design – scale and proportion. As a general guide, the more room you have the larger you can go with your plant choices.

Think about the interior style of your home. Is it traditional, modern, bohemian or something totally different? What colour scheme and furnishings do you have? Be honest about how you use space in your home, too. There's no point keeping delicate plants on a coffee table if kids or pets are going to knock them over.

SHOP

When you're clear on what space you have and what kind of plants you like, it's time to make your selection. Be sure to hold on to any care information you are given about your new plants.

STYLE

Dedicate some time to this part so that you can enjoy the process without being rushed. Team your new plants with their pots or vessels and position them in their allocated spots throughout your home. Now sit back and enjoy the result!

EXPERT TIP

My favourite plant to style with is an indoor plant that's actually a part of the cactus family from Brazil. It was the dazzling hot-pink flowers that first attracted me (like many birds) to the Christmas cactus; however, once the flowers dropped, I was even more taken with the incredible, almost skeletal, branches. Its jointed segments have the ability to look almost prehistoric yet completely contemporary at the same time. It's also dead easy to look after – a plus for the botanically challenged like me.

Heather Nette King, interior stylist and writer

Boston fern and devil's ivy

Hoya heuschkeliana, Christmas cactus and Chinese money plant

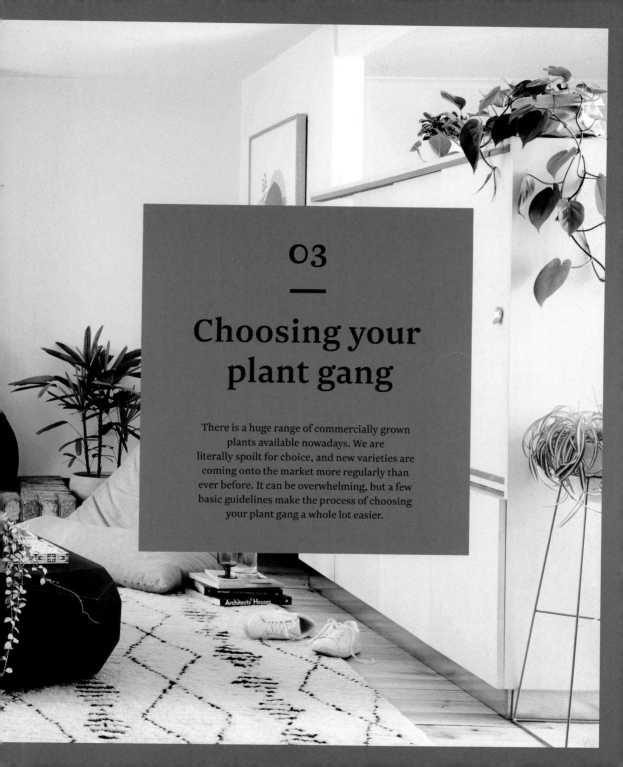

03

—

Choosing your plant gang

There is a huge range of commercially grown plants available nowadays. We are literally spoilt for choice, and new varieties are coming onto the market more regularly than ever before. It can be overwhelming, but a few basic guidelines make the process of choosing your plant gang a whole lot easier.

What to look for

GROWTH PATTERNS

Before committing to a plant, think about its size and how it will grow. Some indoor plants do most of their growing before they are made available to buy. For example, a kentia palm can take up to six years to reach a height of two metres. If you're in the market for a large plant, it makes sense to buy a well-established one from a nursery rather than trying to grow it at home. It also allows you to choose the height you want: nurseries often have an assortment of specimens for people who prefer small or medium-sized plants.

Small, sparse, one-stemmed plants will not grow into large multiple-stemmed specimens without the help of repotting and propagation. Buy the bushiest, fullest specimen you can.

Many indoor plants, like heartleaf philodendrons, umbrella plants and fiddle leaf figs, will keep growing steadily after you take them home. Every plant is different, so it pays to do a little research before making a purchase. You can encourage growth by repotting in spring when the plant is ready. Signs that a plant needs to be repotted include roots appearing through drainage holes or a network of fine roots visible on the surface. Only ever go up one pot size at a time. If your plant is particularly fragile, old or isn't showing clear signs of needing repotting but the soil looks cracked, tired and lacklustre, you can top-dress with potting mix. Gently scrape away the top few centimetres of soil – making sure you don't damage the root ball – then replace it with fresh potting mix.

HEALTHY PLANTS

Plants are highly resilient but don't purchase plants that show signs of distress, as this often means they've experienced less than ideal conditions. To ensure your plant has the best start in life, choose healthy, thriving specimens so your investment in them is well spent.

Choose plants that have lots of new buds, moist soil and perky leaves. Signs of new growth are always good. Avoid plants with yellowing or dead leaves or bare and tired looking stems. It often pays to carefully compare the choices on offer. Choose a plant with as many stems as possible for your budget. Sometimes the same plant can be sold with one stem or three – you're simply getting more for your money.

Umbrella plant

FLOWERS

Flowering plants like peperomia 'Rosso' and peace lily are often sold while they are in flower to showcase their eye-catching blooms. The flowers can last months, but they will eventually die off. If you keep the plant in ideal conditions you can expect it to flower again, though this can sometimes be harder to achieve at home.

The great thing is that even when the flowers are gone, the beauty of the plant remains. If your plant isn't in flower when you buy it, ask if it has flowered recently or when it might be going to. It comes down to personal choice – whether or not your brand new plant has flowers won't usually affect its ability to thrive.

PLANT SIZE

Scale and proportion – two basic principles of interior design – should always be considered when working with plants. As a general guide, the more room you have the larger you can go with your plant choices, but it really comes down to the overall look and how the plants relate to the other items in your home.

Small plants are those in pots that are 5–13cm in diameter. Examples are radiator plant, hoya, mistletoe cacti and air plants. These plants are the ideal size to sit on shelves, tables and windowsills. Petite plants like chain of hearts can have delicate, pretty leaves, but there are also larger, more sculptural types that are still considered a 'small plant'. Devil's ivy has much bigger leaves but it can be potted in a small pot. A single plant variety can also be found in a range of different pot sizes. Peacock plants are often used in terrariums when they are young, but they are also a popular medium-sized pot plant when they are more established.

Small plants are best used where they can be seen. It's no good putting a tiny air plant on a busy wall unit that is awash with books and decor items – the effect will be lost. Choose a location where the plant can be the main focus. A bedside, desktop or bathroom counter is ideal. Get creative with your positioning too. Even one strategically placed plant can have a big effect. Small plants with long tendrils, like chain of hearts, can also have an overall visual effect that is equal to a much larger plant.

Fruit salad plant, rubber plant and umbrella plant

Medium-sized plants are generally 15–30cm in potted diameter. They're ideal for placing on the floor, in plant stands or on top of suitably large furniture like TV cabinets, tables or dressers. Almost every room has a spot that is too small for furniture but too large to leave bare – this is exactly where a medium-sized plant comes into its own. They can brighten a dull corner, fill an empty set of shelves or create a beautiful eye-level scene that captures your attention. Umbrella plant, fruit salad plant and rubber plant are popular choices.

If you have the space, large potted plants (more than 30cm in diameter) are a great asset to any interior. They help make the most of space, create a visual journey for the eye to linger on, and can soften stark designs in a home. Wide-reaching varieties can also be used to create interesting focal points and dramatic scenes. Umbrella plant, cacti, kentia palm and fiddle leaf fig are good examples. Don't forget that larger-leafed plants catch a lot of dust. This can reduce their ability to absorb light and grow. Wipe them regularly with a soft, damp cloth, being careful not to damage the leaves.

Umbrella plant, kentia palm and fiddle leaf fig

What plants need

LIGHT

Light is a key consideration when choosing your plants, as a plant without light will simply not survive. In Australia, north-facing windows get the most light during the year. (In the northern hemisphere, this is a south-facing position.) Most indoor plants will grow well in filtered northern light or – better still – near an east or west-facing window, which is the sweet spot for our green-leafed friends. Good plants for spots with filtered light are weeping fig, bird of paradise, umbrella plant and hoya.

The strength of the sunlight changes with the seasons. In winter and autumn, plants in a sunny north-facing position often enjoy morning sunlight, but in summer the midday sun can be so intense it can scorch their leaves. Good plants for sunny spots are string of pearls, spider plant, snake plant, succulents and cacti. Some varieties of plants are adept at tolerating the low-light conditions that are often found in south-facing spots. Devil's ivy, cast iron plant, mistletoe cacti, zanzibar gem and peace lily are all hardy options. Having said that, they will also thrive if they are given more light. In very dark locations, you can move the plant to a brighter spot for a few hours every other day to help its growth.

Bird of paradise, weeping fig and umbrella plant

Maidenhair fern and Chinese money plant

TEMPERATURE AND HUMIDITY

Most houseplants like a temperature range between 18 and 23 °C, which is easily achieved in most modern homes. The amount of moisture in the air, known as humidity, is a little harder to control. To check the humidity level in your home, you can use an instrument called a hygrometer, which can be bought at hardware stores. Alternatively, there are visual indicators you can look out for. High humidity is often characterised by condensation on the inside of windows, wet stains on walls and even mould. Low humidity is more prevalent during the winter months when temperatures are cooler and heating is used often. Signs of low humidity can include persistent sore throats or dry skin, increased frequency of static electricity shocks from touching metal or synthetic objects and even peeling wallpaper.

If the air in your home is very dry, mist your plants daily first thing in the morning before the sun or heating system starts to warm up the house. You can also sit plants on trays of small pebbles covered in water. Keep the water just below the top of the pebbles so the plant does not soak up any water and remains well aerated. You can buy humidity trays specifically for this purpose. Humidifiers, which add moisture to the air, and dehumidifiers, which remove it, can also help to rectify any issues you're facing.

Check the humidity requirements of your individual plants. Plants that enjoy high humidity include maidenhair fern, air plants and Chinese money plant. Keep a close eye on them and if you see signs of dryness, or they start to look lacklustre, increase humidity levels using the tactics above.

FOOD

Every plant needs a mix of three main chemical elements to thrive: nitrogen, phosphorus and potassium. These nutrients are all found in plant fertiliser. When you bring a plant home from the nursery, it will have fertiliser in its soil or potting mix already. These nutrients will be gradually used up so they will need to be replaced.

As a guide, feed plants in soil-based mixture every three months and soil-less plants, like succulents and cacti, every six to eight weeks. However, make sure to only feed the plant during its growth periods: spring and summer. If you feed a plant during its rest period you can damage it. Choose a complete fertiliser that is best suited to your plants – there are lots on the market.

Chain of hearts, krimson princess hoya and air plants

04

Plant accessories

Not only are there hundreds of plants to choose from, there is also an exciting array of plant accessories to work with. The golden rule is that your accessories should complement your plants rather than overwhelm them. The plants are the real stars here.

Krimson queen hoya, krimson princess hoya, devil's ivy and air plant

POTS

Everyone has probably owned a terracotta pot, but there are many more materials being used to hold plants nowadays: ceramic, cement, stoneware, fibreglass, seagrass – even washable paper bags. The options are endless.

When you are choosing a pot for a new plant, think about how you are going to use it. Check the size of the plastic container your plant has come in then look for a new pot that it will fit in. You can either plant directly into the new pot, or keep the plant in the plastic container and use the new pot as a cache-pot (a decorative container that holds a plant pot). If you're going to plant directly into the new pot, let the plant settle into your home for a couple of weeks before doing so – repotting too soon may send your plant into shock and kill it. The best time to repot is during the start of the plant's active growth period, which is generally in spring. Also, only ever increase your pot size by two inches width and/or depth at a time – a pot that's too big gives the roots too much space to grow into. The plant won't grow above the soil until its roots begin to fill the container. An oversized pot can also hold excessive amounts of water and cause root rot.

Variegated monstera

DRAINAGE

It's a good idea to use a drip tray when you have a pot with drainage holes. This will catch any drips and also allows you to water the plant without having to move it to a sink or put it outside. Drip trays can be hidden inside larger pots or put on display as a design feature. Empty any excess water from the tray. Some plants can survive without drainage and – given the array of beautifully designed vessels that are available – you might be tempted to go that way. If you've decided to put a plant into a pot without drainage holes, be very careful with your watering. Only let a little bit of water in at a time and keep it to a minimum. If there is too much water, tip the pot on its side to drain. The last thing you want to do is drown your plant. Another option is to use self-watering pots, which have a well in their base to store water. These are great if you're a regular traveller or a bit forgetful.

A grouping of plants including fiddle leaf fig, *hoya odetteae* and green exotica hoya

Now the real fun begins. Do you have a penchant for handmade, one-of-a-kind pots? Do you prefer textured or smooth finishes, bold or muted colours, simple or elaborate shapes? Work out what appeals to you, how well the pot will complement your plant, and if the pot will fit in with the overall look of your home.

If you are working with a delicate plant, try a light-coloured container with a simple shape. Pair a plant that has a strong, sculptural shape or bold colours with a visually striking vessel for an amplified effect or, for a softer look, choose a simpler pot. Large plants often work well with bold containers, like painted or patterned pots, where the plant isn't swamped by the loudness of the pattern.

You can be brave with patterns and colours, or stick to a muted, softer palette of greys and blacks that will work in almost any space. Don't forget to think about where the potted plant will sit in your home. Some contrast between the plant and the wall behind it can be visually striking. Light-coloured walls can also help plants by reflecting more light around the room. A dark wall often makes a poor backdrop for a dark pot and plant, unless you are deliberately going for a moody look and don't mind the greenery not being the focus.

Pots that can be used both indoors and outdoors give you more flexibility in how and where you use them. If you get tired of them inside, pop them outdoors with a different plant for an entirely fresh look. Choose a neutral shade so they can work in a variety of locations over time.

EXPERT TIP

I tend to select plants based on the softness I can imagine them adding to a space. I like plants that are not so much structured, but whimsical and loose. I choose plants that have a consistency in colour tone. I also like an indoor climber!

Simone Haag, designer and stylist

Spath sensation, kentia palm, devil's ivy and maidenhair fern

PLANT STANDS

Plant stands were very popular in the 1970s and have recently enjoyed a resurgence. Stands are a great way to give your plants extra height and prominence, plus they are a flexible way to decorate your home with plants. Many plant stands offer multiple ways to display your greenery.

There are now an array of modern designs, shapes and colours to choose from. Neutrals like black and white are always a safe bet, but always think about how the stand will complement the pot and plant. You can often get away with using a feature colour – plant stands are only a decor accessory so you can afford to be bold.

Remember to consider the kind of pots and plants you are going to use with your stands. Upright and trailing specimens can create surprisingly different looks in the same plant stand. Play around with the options until you find the perfect solution to complement your plant choice.

PLANT HANGERS AND SHELVES

When you're short on space, maximise what you have by thinking vertically. There's a huge range of plant hangers and shelves with inbuilt plant pots on the market. Made from a wide range of materials – powder-coated steel, wood, ceramic, recycled plastic and even salvaged materials – these versatile accessories work exceptionally well in small spaces like bathrooms and ensuites.

Although they are usually hung from the ceiling, plant hangers can also be suspended from wall hooks and even shelving units (just make sure they can take the weight). Some plant stands are also specially designed to hold plant hangers, offering another unique way to display your plants.

Chinese money plant, mistletoe cactus and variegated *hoya heuschkeliana*

TERRARIUMS

Known for their ease-of-care and uncanny beauty, the glorious glass worlds of terrariums have become very popular. Operating as an encapsulated eco-system, these transparent microsystems require no water as long as they remain closed at all times.

Terrariums – and mossariums, which are planted with moss only – are one-of-a-kind living sculptures that come in a variety of different sizes, shapes and finishes with bases and lids of marble, wood, and even cork.

Given their low maintenance needs, terrariums are a great option for people who are short on time or who aren't able to care for more needy plants.

Whether your interior style is contemporary, nostalgic, brutal or colourfully bold, there is a plant that will add to it. Look at the shape first – is it graphic or rounded? Lush or minimal? Match your plants to your decor style and they will always add a wonderful organic dimension to a room.

Heather Nette King, interior stylist and writer

STRING GARDENS

String gardens are a contemporary version of the traditional Japanese kokedama – a ball of moss-covered soil on which an ornamental plant grows. String gardens are kokedama with an additional layer of polyfelt that protects and insulates the ball, and keeps it much neater (kokedama often shed their moss as they grow).

String gardens are usually created with plants like devil's ivy or *Rhipsalis* varieties. As well as being a striking and artful way to display plants, they can last for years.

String gardens can be used with plant stands or hung from the ceiling, wall or even shelves. Caring for them is easy: simply submerge the ball in water for ten minutes every ten days, leave it to drip outside in the shade for a short time and then bring it back in. Plant care doesn't get much simpler.

STAKES

Plant stakes can play an integral role in the healthy growth of plants that have long slender stems, which droop if they are not well supported. Stakes can also add a design element to potted plants, showcasing the natural beauty of trailing plants and turning them into vertical works of art.

EXPERT TIP

Plants bring a sense of life and soul into an interior.
Having a touch of the outdoors inside makes such
an impact on our everyday lives.

Steve Cordony, interior stylist

AIR PLANT HOLDERS

Air plant holders have been around for years, but today's designs have a very different look and feel to those of the past. Where there used to be a focus on natural supports, like wooden branches covered with moss and groups of plants, today's holders are much simpler and focus on supporting a single plant. The use of materials like metal, brass and ceramics allow the air plant to be the star of the show.

Air plants

As their name suggests, air plants – widely varying forms of bromeliad, also known as *Tillandsia* – don't need soil to grow. In the wild, they attach themselves to other plants. They absorb moisture and nutrients through their leaves so they do still need to be watered.

Watering

Mist spray two or three times a week. Spanish moss can be submerged in water for ten minutes a week.

Light

Bright filtered light is best but no direct sun, as they'll scorch.

Styling tip

Air plants add another dimension to your styling, as they provide a very different shape to potted plants. They can also be used in a number of different scenarios – hanging, attached to a wall hook, in an air plant holder or even showcased as a collection in a low bowl for maximum impact.

05
—
Plant styling principles

There are a few simple principles when it comes to
styling with plants that you'll come across again
and again. Once you get the hang of them, they
become second nature and the whole process gets
easier. Practice really does make perfect, so don't
be afraid to have a go!

RECOGNISING SHAPES

There are five basic plant shapes, each with their own special beauty. Learning to recognise these shapes helps you create interesting groupings where the plants complement each other. For instance, pairing a bushy or trailing plant with a tree can soften the overall look, while an upright plant can add a striking and bold sculptural element.

Don't forget that plants are living things that change as they grow. Before you take a plant home, consider the shape of the plant and how it might change over time. Will the shape stay the same? If not, will it still work in your home?

Mexican snow ball

ROSETTE

A rosette is a predominantly circular arrangement of leaves that are mostly at the same height. Foliage grows directly from the crown of the plant and can often look like flowers. Rosettes can make a striking single display alone or they can be used with other shapes to create an interesting contrast. Some examples are Mexican snow ball, century plant, bromeliads, bird's nest fern and a number of air plants.

BUSHY

Bushy plants are often as wide as they are tall and have many stems growing from their base. Their solid appearance makes them helpful for creating a green backdrop. They're also very handy for hiding things like electrical cords or sockets on a wall. Some examples include maidenhair fern, kentia palm, Chinese money plant, lady palm and happy plant.

Kentia palm

Weeping fig

TREE-LIKE

Tree-like plants typically have a single trunk with branches and leaves at the top. They can be very effective for styling. It's often best to just use one, so that its shape and character can be appreciated, but if you're keen to maximise your plant gang there's no rule that says they can't also work as a group. Some examples are fiddle leaf fig, rubber tree, weeping fig and fig tree.

Devil's ivy

UPRIGHT

Upright plants grow straight up and make a striking contrast to other plants. Single uprights work well with a smaller trailing, rosette or bushy plant to soften the overall look. Upright plants also look very effective when different varieties are grouped together. The unique intricacies of each plant can be easily appreciated amongst the overarching upright theme. Some examples are snake plant, African milk tree, giant bird of paradise and peace lily.

CLIMBING AND TRAILING

Climbing and trailing plants often have thin, curling leaf stems that search out the next spot to cling to. Put simply, they go where you tell them to go. They can cascade down a set of shelves, wind themselves vertically around a stake or climb across a bathroom wall. The options are endless. Some examples are devil's ivy, heartleaf philodendron and varieties of hoya, which can both climb and trail. Donkey's tail and mistletoe cacti are also good trailing options.

GROUPING PLANTS

A single plant can look fantastic, but the power of plants really springs to life when they're grouped together. There are a million ways to group plants, but remember to consider each plant's suitability for that area of your home. You want all the plants in your group to thrive and look great.

There are four key elements to consider when choosing your grouping: colour, shape, texture and variety. Choose one as your focus. Too many contrasts in a display can be confusing. But don't feel that you have to be bound by these suggestions. Sometimes bending the rules can create something extra special.

COLOUR

You can stick to the same or different shades of green, or even add the contrast of a red-tipped leaf or the vibrancy of a flowering succulent. Very dark leaves can look black, adding interest to a group and working well in contemporary spaces when green is not ideal. Variegated plants offer unique foliage colours too.

Ensure the colours you choose don't clash or compete with each other for attention, and always consider the plant's location within your home. For example, a ruby rubber plant with its bold shades of pink and cream could appear entirely at odds against bright, patterned wallpaper.

Snake plant, rubber plant, ribbon plant, spath sensation and chain of hearts.

SHAPE

A display can be vertical, horizontal, triangular or even circular, depending on where it sits in your home, what containers you use and what works best in a particular space. A vertical arrangement is a great starting point and can often be used in multiple scenarios. Choose one tall plant to lead the group, add a shorter, bushier one and then complement those with a small plant or two that have some looseness.

TEXTURE

Play around with the contrast between rough and undulating leaves or smooth and glossy foliage. Subtle textural differences will add dimension and emphasise the different shades of green in any grouping. Textural delight can also come from your vessels and pots. Contrast rough and smooth surfaces, carved ceramic detailing, or even fabrics, paper and woven knits.

the stylists guide to

VARIETY

Strength in numbers is a strong statement. Closely related plant varieties, like different cacti or succulents or even trailing plants, can create an interesting and cohesive scene.

An assortment of plants in the Ivy Muse store

CREATING A LOOK

Plants have a unique ability to add dimension to your decorating style at a fraction of the cost of the latest 'must have' accessory. Some plants are associated with certain fashions, locations or vibes and you can use this to create a distinctive look that echoes the style of your home, or to create contrasting scenes.

Here, the same interior space is styled in four different ways. Simple pots keep the focus on the plants.

COASTAL

Plants that are commonly found in coastal landscapes can conjure up a tropical, beachside feeling. You can create a striking look with just a few of these plant varieties.

Giant bird of paradise, spath sensation and lady palm

Moonshine snake plant, mistletoe cactus, snowdrop cactus, zanzibar gem, fig tree and zebra plant (calathea)

CONTEMPORARY

For a fresh contemporary look, choose unusual plants that have an interesting silhouette. Play with height and shape to create an exciting visual feast and think outside the box when it comes to vessels. Pair a large tree with a canvas basket for a contemporary take on a classic pot or try a metal stand to round out the styling and add another dimension to the group.

Fruit salad plant and rubber plant

MINIMALIST

The trick here is to employ the idea that 'less is more' by using fewer plants and choosing bold varieties. Large leaves with interesting shapes have loads of visual presence.

BOHEMIAN

To evoke a bohemian jungle vibe, go for maximum impact and choose plants that have a variety of sizes and textures. A layered look is very effective. Place some plants on the ground and use stands and supports at different heights to create visual links.

Christmas cactus, green exotica hoya, *hoya heuschkeliana*, spider plant, golden cane palm, fruit salad plant and Boston fern

CREATING A
GREEN VIGNETTE

A vignette is an arrangement of objects that tell a story and green vignettes have the added beauty of plant life. Vignettes are the bread and butter of the styling profession. They have become even more popular recently – probably because they are perfect for sharing on image-based social media apps like Instagram and Pinterest. Creating a green vignette is a great way to practice your styling prowess and tell your own unique story.

The first thing to do is choose a flat, steady surface to work with. Dressers, sideboards and drawers are a great starting point. Small and medium-sized vignettes work well on shelves, tabletops or even bench seats. Single plants can sometimes look lost, so they often look better on windowsills or small side tables where they aren't swamped by their surroundings. If your vignette sits above eye level, perhaps on a shelf, cascading plant tendrils will have more impact than an upright plant that won't easily be seen from below.

From there, collect an assortment of plants and other objects that have some meaning for you and begin building a story. You can stick to an all-green theme, or add a few knick-knacks to complement the plants you've chosen. Use the golden rules below to help you plan and create your vignette but remember that the key is to let the plants take centre stage!

TRIANGLES

Vignettes that create a soft, asymmetrical triangular shape are ideal. Our eyes like to flow over scenes and this shape helps the arrangement appear uncontrived. It's perfect for an informal, relaxed look. A tall plant at the back gives the scene height, and smaller plants on either side create the triangular shape. A trailing plant adds texture and looseness to the overall look.

Bunny ear cactus, African milk tree, string of pearls and Chinese money plant

Emerald ripple, fruit salad plant and prayer plant

RULE OF THREE

An uneven number of items – three, five, seven, nine or more – often works best when you are creating a vignette. Odd-numbered arrangements are pleasing to the eye as they are less studied and, when done correctly, have an effortless vibe. Vignettes with even numbers can appear formal, tight and a bit old-fashioned.

You don't have to be bound by this rule though. Sometimes, because of their positioning, four items may look like three. When you start to play around with creating vignettes, you'll start to see how this works. But if you're unsure, just stick to odd numbers until you get the hang of it.

ADD SOME ART

Get your vignettes to work harder by matching them with art or other objects on the wall to maximise their overall height. Tall, slim plants work well as they draw the eye up from the scene and encompass the art, giving you more bang for your buck. And the added bonus? You'll be able to appreciate these vignettes from the other side of the room.

Emerald ripple, umbrella plant and krimson queen hoya

SPACE

The use of space can make or break a vignette. Try bunching the items in a group with a little layering. You could have one overlapping another when the vignette is viewed from the front. The key is to have one item that sits by itself and has some breathing room around it. It doesn't have to sit so far away that it looks like it doesn't belong, just enough so that you can see its silhouette.

Emerald ripple, mini monstera and royal Hawaiian hoya

Firestick plant, mountain aloe, white ghost cactus and bunny ear cactus

COLOUR

Colour can elicit an emotional response, especially when used in our homes. Blue and green are perceived to be calming, while red and yellow are recognised for their stimulating effect. Being in the centre of the spectrum, green is the colour of balance. It meets the eye in a way that requires no visual adjustment whatsoever and is, therefore, restful.

Colour also affects the flow of a vignette and can play a huge role in how effective it is; if colours are clashing it will simply not look good. Make sure that the items and vessels in the vignette complement your plants. The most complementary colours for greenery include neutrals (black, white, greys, browns), soft pastels (nude, mint, peach, light blue) and varying shades of terracotta. Heavily saturated colours can often compete for attention with the plants, making the vignette look disjointed.

THE WORLD OF CHARLES AND RAY EAMES

barbican

06

—

Styling solutions for every room

Different rooms in your home may need different treatments, depending on how you use them, how much time you spend in them or how much light or heat they get. Use plants that have a consistent theme or vibe, or go wild and mix up your plant choices to allow the plants themselves to be the overarching theme. Follow your heart and you won't go wrong.

BEDROOMS

You spend almost a third of your life tucked up in bed, so your bedroom should be a tranquil place to rest and recuperate. By reminding us of our connection with nature, plants help create a peaceful space that encourages relaxation and calmness.

Whether it's a simple potted plant on a bedside table or a jungle-like boudoir with a wild mix of greenery, every bedroom will benefit from a touch of green.

PLACEMENT

Think outside the box when it comes to placing your plants. Bench seats provide flat space while remaining completely functional. They also break up the look of tall beds and add an interesting focal point to the room.

Side tables and stools of different heights create a staggered effect that gives each plant its own visual space. To maximise your plant display footprint, choose a side table with a cupboard or inbuilt shelves to hold your personal effects. Free up space for plants on your bedside table by swapping a bedside lamp for pendant lighting and consider a small plant like emerald ripple or Chinese money plant.

Fiddle leaf fig, zanzibar gem, fan aloe, heartleaf philodendron and fruit salad plant

Air plants, chain of hearts and flowers

LIGHTING

If your bedroom suffers from low light conditions, plants like a parlour palm or peace lily are good choices. If you're lucky enough to have an east-facing bedroom, you have more options.

PRIVACY

Used in the right way, plants can offer some privacy when your neighbour's window is a mere few metres away from your own. A few small plants on the windowsill, like a trailing chain of hearts or sculptural air plant, draws your attention from the view outside.

In larger bedrooms, bigger plants like the broad-leafed fiddle leaf fig can be placed near a window. It's a win–win situation: the plant will love its bright position and you will wake up to a green scene every morning.

EVERY BEDROOM NEEDS A BIG PLANT

Floor space in a bedroom can sometimes be tight, but there are often
large blank walls. The solution is a big plant – anywhere from two
metres upwards will do. There are heaps of big plants to choose
from, and you can even use a plant stand to increase the height.
Choose a plant that has a lot going on up top (the wider the better),
but has a slim footprint. Ideally, you want to put it in a spot where it is
out of the way. Next to the bed is a good option if you have the space.
Just make sure you won't bump into it in the dark.

Wax flowers

There are nearly 200 species of hoya, sometimes known as wax flowers. Originally from tropical Asia and Australasia, these woody-stemmed vines have delicate porcelain-like flowers and lustrous evergreen foliage. They thrive in warmer conditions and enjoy a bright spot.

Watering

Keep moist in warmer months and drier in winter and you can expect to have a beautiful plant for many years.

Light

Three to four hours of direct sunlight are required every day for healthy growth and flowering.

Styling tip

You can use hoya to create interesting sculptural shapes. Each one has its own unique character – we've never seen two exactly alike! We have a particular fondness for their versatility, their uniquely shaped leaves and the beautiful shades of green they offer.

Favourite varieties

Krimson queen hoya, *Hoya heuschkeliana* and green exotica hoya all cast wonderful trailing silhouettes.

BATHROOMS

Bathrooms are generally the simplest room in a house and, to be honest, they can be a bit boring. Yet they're also one of the most used areas, so it pays to give them a little extra attention. As well as adding texture and interest, plants can thrive in a bathroom. Unlike decor pieces that might suffer from the moist conditions, they love a bit of humidity.

Bathrooms are notoriously hard to decorate. You might have a cute stool, a beautiful towel or two and some designer soap, but what else can you add? There's often too much stark, blank space and too few interesting focal points. This is where plants come in. Even the smallest of plants can help soften the space, breathe some life into it and complete the scene. Even the most stunning of bathrooms will benefit from a little plant love.

Zanzibar gem, mistletoe cactus, krimson princess hoya, green exotica hoya and chain of hearts

SIZE

Bathrooms are usually small, but think of this as an opportunity rather than a problem, and get creative with greenery. Take a good hard look at your bathroom. Does it have a high ledge, a windowsill or a perfectly placed ceiling hook that you've never used? Elements like these can be used to display your plants. And don't forget accessories like plant hangers – they can be used to great effect in small spaces. Choose suitable plants, and remember that even one small plant can make a huge difference.

Use neutral pots to keep the focus on the greenery and the details of the bathroom. Sticking to light colours also helps to make a space feel larger and more open. Darker pots and plants make it feel smaller and more intimate.

If you're lucky enough to have a large bathroom, your options for adding plants really open up. Single, large potted trees or a grouped selection can create a dramatic and lush environment that will make you feel as if you are bathing in the jungle.

Leatherleaf fern

PLACEMENT

In small bathrooms, focus on making the most of your space. Hang air plants on the wall, fill windowsills with a mix of pots and place medium-sized plants on the floor to help break up the space. Think about how the plants will grow. If the space is limited, choose plants that grow vertically or will cascade down a wall rather than spreading out horizontally.

Check the light conditions to make sure you are either choosing plants that enjoy bright light or grow well in more shaded positions.

GOING FULL JUNGLE

If you're keen on creating a jungle-like vibe in your bathroom, think outside the box. Bathrooms tend to have limited floor space so consider using the vertical space above with plant hangers or creeping vines. A single plant hanger can be very effective used on its own but, if space allows, try more.

If you are using the same kind of plants, stagger the heights of the planters. If you have chosen a mixture of trailing and upright plants, keep the hangers at the same height. Either method will create a flowing vignette with a soft triangular shape and stop the look from being overly formal or structured.

Fruit salad plant

THREE PLANTS THAT WILL THRIVE IN A BATHROOM

Our top three plants for bathrooms are begonia, fruit salad plant and peace lily. Begonia and peace lily don't like dry conditions, so the humidity of a bathroom is ideal. All three are easy to care for. Begonia and fruit salad plant enjoy filtered light while peace lilies grow well in medium light, which is great if your bathroom verges on the shady side. During the warmer months, when they are growing, allow the top few centimetres of potting mix to dry out before watering again. In winter, water more sparingly – depending on the moisture levels in your bathroom, this may mean not much watering at all.

Begonia silver jewel

Zanzibar gem and mistletoe cactus

DARK BATHROOMS

Bathrooms often have very little or no natural light at all. It's a problem – indoor plants really do need some light to thrive. If there is a little bit of light, try a devil's ivy or heartleaf philodendron. They are both trailing and climbing plants, so they work well in a variety of positions. If you need an upright option, go with a zanzibar gem, commonly known as the plant that 'thrives on neglect'. If there's no absolutely no light, focus your efforts on the rooms in your home that have windows or skylights instead!

KITCHENS

The kitchen can often be a hive of activity, as well as the heart of a home. It's a place where family and friends meet to cook, share meals and spend quality time. Today, kitchens are increasingly multifunctional spaces. Kids can be found doing homework while the parents cook, dining tables double as a desk for work-from-home entrepreneurs and, if you're throwing a party, everyone will be in the kitchen – whether you planned it that way or not!

Kitchens are usually a great spot for houseplants. Most plants enjoy bright conditions that are out of direct sunlight, and kitchens usually have at least one of these spots. There's also generally space for plants to spread out – shelves, windowsills, benches, cabinetry or, at the very least, the top of the fridge.

But the kitchen's real secret to successfully housing plants is that we are in it a lot, every day. The key to keeping your plants thriving is to check them regularly. With so much time spent in and out of the kitchen, this becomes second nature.

PLANNING

Before you start styling your kitchen with plants, think about how you use the space and what you would like to achieve. Do you just want to add some touches of greenery or go all-out with a jungle theme? Consider your space and what will work well. If you want to use large, spreading plants, you'll need enough space for them to grow horizontally. If you've only got room on a bench or table, look for plants that are suited to that. Identify the places where plants could sit – the goal is to complement rather than overwhelm. There should be a purpose and reason for every plant and its placement, even if it's just because you love to look at it.

Variegated *hoya heuschkeliana* and umbrella plant

Rosemary, basil and parsley

PLACEMENT

Big kitchen benches or tables can be functionally great when you're cooking but, when you aren't using them, they can look barren and boring. Try adding a plant with height to give the bench a focal point. Make sure it's easy to move when you need to use the space again.

Large enclosed terrariums also work well. They are low-maintenance, self-watering, and the wooden ones won't scratch delicate marble or stone benchtops when you move them. There are lots of great small businesses making terrariums these days or, if you're creatively inclined, you can have a go at making one yourself. There's plenty of advice to be found online or in books.

If you are a keen cook, a bright spot like a windowsill is the perfect place for potted herbs. They will grow well and be easily accessible when you are cooking.

Styling a kitchen table

Kitchen and dining tables are big, flat and easy spots to add greenery to. Take advantage of this well-placed platform to showcase a single plant, a small grouping or a green-themed tablescape.

WEEKDAY

For day-to-day greenery, it makes sense to have something that's easy to care for, low-maintenance and doesn't take up too much room. A mix of small ceramic pots and succulents can be teamed with a couple of ceramic trinkets for interest. Small potted plants can work well too.

A mix of succulents with Japanese andromeda

WEEKEND

Just as you often change the way you use your table, you can also switch up the plant life that lives on it. An easy way to spruce it up on your weekend is to add a bunch of fresh blooms. Go for varieties that have predominantly white buds and green foliage – this gives them a visual link to the plants they are sitting with.

Hoya odettea, delphinium, viburnum foliage and solomon seal

ROMANTIC

To create a romantic, feminine scene, start with a soft trailing plant and a selection of pretty green and white flowers. Plant stands add height and presence and the display can be rounded out by a cute ceramic vase and some florals. Plants and flowers used together create a botanical delight.

CONTEMPORARY

Glass cloches are a modern yet simple way to display a collection of air plants. Choose coloured glass that complements your decor or opt for clear glass to showcase more of the plant's detail. Add single supported air plants to create a scene that showcases the plant's graphic form.

An arrangement of air plants

Jitters, emerald ripple, button fern, *hoya heuschkeliana* and chain of hearts

SCANDI

Start with a base of neutral pots and vessels of varying textures, shapes and heights. The key is to keep the theme neutral and the colour palette consistent. Be creative with your plant choices. Different plant silhouettes and unique leaf shapes cut a striking figure and create an arrangement full of interest and movement.

Chinese money plant

The Chinese money plant has become one of the most sought-after plants in recent times, especially in Australia where it is relatively new on the scene. This adorable and prolific plant is a bit of a wonder in botanical circles. Botanists only identified it in the 1980s; however, many amateur gardeners had already cultivated the plant at home. When thriving, the Chinese money plant grows small basal shoots which are easily harvested and can be shared among friends – a truly heartwarming example of plants connecting people.

Watering

Moderate water through the warmer season. Be sure to let the surface soil dry out between waterings.

Light

A versatile plant suited to medium to filtered lighting conditions.

Styling tip

Team with a neutral pot to let its beautiful leaves remain the focal point.

BORING CORNERS

Boring corners are often screaming out for plants. Whether you create a full-on display using a whole heap of plants, or simply add a small group of plants to the area, you can transform that dull corner into something worth noticing. Large plants are particularly good in corners, as they can stretch out without getting in the way. And, if you have the space, a gang of plants lead by a large plant can be an incredible sight.

LIVING ROOMS

The living room is usually one of the biggest rooms in a house and it meets a lot of needs. It's used for hanging out, relaxing and entertaining guests. It has to be inspiring yet relaxing, comfortable yet memorable and, of course, always a pleasure to spend time in. The key to styling your living room is to get to grips with its special features. Does it have period details, a wonderful neutral backdrop or plenty of open-plan space? Living rooms, especially when they are filled with great decor items like sofas, rugs and artworks, are an exciting opportunity to style with plants and create something magical.

PLACEMENT

When it comes to styling with plants, the living room has a few helpful tricks up its sleeve. There are often a lot of surfaces to create arrangements on and floor space to work with as well. Picture rails and fireplace mantles are like gold-dust to stylists – if your home has them, make good use of them! Hang plants from picture rails or train climbers across them. Mantles look great with a plant or two, or you could create a jungle.

Mistletoe cactus, heartleaf philodendron, prayer plant, air plant, devil's ivy and krimson queen hoya

OPEN PLAN

Open-plan living rooms are a perfect scenario for large plants like the fiddle leaf fig and kentia palm. Plants like these are particularly good for softening stark and modern spaces and linking large spaces together. Restrain yourself though – only use one or two rather than create a heaving collection which might detract from their overall attractiveness.

STYLING A LOUNGE ROOM

The focal point of this room is the large, dark fireplace. The fig tree,
rhapis palm and trailing plants have a softening effect, drawing the eye not
just to the fireplace but also to the pockets of greenery. The heavy look of
the coffee table and couch is broken up by the light-coloured variegated
hoya heuschkeliana and krimson queen hoya. The spider plant on the
stand livens up the blank wall and adds another point of interest.

Plant Style

EXPERT TIP

I love styling with large indoor plants and making them a focal point of a room. Plants that almost touch the ceiling add drama and scale that you can't get from furniture.

Steve Cordony, interior stylist

Satin pothos, fruit salad plant, swiss cheese vine and Indian rope hoya

STYLING A COFFEE TABLE

Stunning tablescapes are created using simple principles like colour
and positioning. Choose a few key plants, then add a couple of
personal items – cute ceramics or a stylish magazine. The contrast
of plants and knick-knacks expresses your personality and creates a
very effective look. Have a consistent colour palette, make sure all
the items have some breathing room and remember that groupings
of three or five objects will generally work better.

Fiddle leaf fig

With its violin-shaped leaves and richly dense tone, the fiddle leaf fig is a popular choice for interior styling. Its popularity has dwindled a bit since it was first in fashion, but it is easy to care for and is very fast growing. And there's no denying that it's a good-looking plant too.

Watering

Water regularly during spring and summer, but let the top layer of soil dry out between waterings. Water sparingly in winter.

Light

Fiddle leaf figs like a brightly lit position, but they can only tolerate direct sun in the morning or during the colder months. Their leaves will scorch in hot summer sun.

Styling tip

Team with a large pot to make a bold statement in any room.

BRIGHTEN UP BLANK WALLS

Make the most of established trailing plants and attach them to wall hooks to create a living, breathing artwork. Drape the plants over wooden wall dots, decorative nails, shelves or even framed artwork.

CREATIVE SPACES

Whether you're running your own business or spending time on your hobby, your creative space should be a nurturing and engaging place. They come in all different sizes and shapes – large studios, small offices and even little nooks tucked away in living rooms and bedrooms. Ultimately, they are a place to feel inspired and motivated in. Fill them with things that make your heart sing, especially plants.

If you can't see the outside world while you're plugging away at work, then bring it inside. According to research by Dr Chris Knight and his fellow psychologists from Exeter University, keeping a plant in your workplace can increase your productivity by fifteen per cent. That sounds like a no brainer to us!

We believe there's a link between creativity and plants too. Plants can be a source of inspiration. Many highly creative people draw upon the rich and rewarding practice of keeping plants to help generate their creative output. Artists paint still lifes with plants nestled amongst the scene, ceramicists create botanical vessels from hand-turned stoneware and musicians craft soulful lyrics conjuring up images of nature.

PLACEMENT

Sometimes space in a work area can be limited, so make the most of what you've got by going vertical. Shelving, wall planters or even plant hangers are all good options. Think outside the box – simple flat-packed shelves or vintage finds can be just as effective as designer pieces. Mix plants with personal items to create layered stories that can offer a little inspiration when you're battling difficult creative problems.

STYLING SHELVES

When choosing plants for shelves, always include at least one hanging option. Introducing a hanging plant to a horizontal shelf automatically adds contrast and texture to an otherwise structured scene. Create an interesting vignette by adding vessels and plants of different shapes and sizes. Sometimes a more restrained approach to creating a vignette can be just as beautiful, if not more functional. Try using your personal objects to tell a story, and complement them with greenery rather than making the plants the focus. Have a play and see what looks best to you. Leave some space to give the plants visual room. Keep an eye on them to check how they're settling into their new home.

Moonshine snake plant

The snake plant, sometimes called mother-in-law's tongue, is very hardy and easy to grow. It has sharp, elongated leaves that stretch upright to create an impressive form. The moonshine variety has very pale green leaves with a slim, dark green border.

Watering

Moderate watering during warm weather. Make sure the soil is completely moistened at each watering, but check that the top of the potting mix is dry before watering again. During the cooler months, allow at least half of the potting mixture to dry out before watering.

Light

This slow-growing plant prefers a sunny position but can also tolerate lower light levels.

Styling tip

An ideal plant when you need to build height within a vignette or group en masse for an impressive display.

STYLING FOR CREATIVE INSPIRATION

A chair nestled amongst plants is a great place to chill out and spark
creative ideas. You don't need a lot of room to create a little haven.
If you're lucky enough to have a bright spot near a window, the
majority of indoor plants will enjoy that position. Just be sure to keep
them out of direct sunlight as they can burn. For darker spots choose
plants that don't mind a little shade, like devil's ivy and zanzibar gem.

SMALL SPOTS

From entryways to mantles, any small space has the potential
to become a focal point within your home. What they often lack
in size, they more than make up for with variety and character.
These nooks and crannies can be a great opportunity for styling
with plants and definitely shouldn't be overlooked. Whether
you want to create a dazzling 'green shelfie' or a windowsill
dripping with a wild assortment of houseplants, it's these little
touches that create a sense of flow from one room to another,
giving a home a sense of unity and an undeniable appreciation
for plant life.

Variegated jade vine and swiss cheese vine

ENTRYWAYS

Though they're rarely a spot we linger in, entryways are a high-traffic area and often the first place visitors see, so it's good to add the welcoming touch of plants. If you have a table, pop a plant or two down to brighten an otherwise boring scenario of keys, coins and trinkets. If you can afford the space, try out medium-sized plants on the floor. If you've got a blank wall, planters can create an alluring spectacle, especially when they are filled with trailing plants.

FIREPLACE MANTLE

Sitting at eye level with plenty of room to play with, fireplace mantles are worth adding into your styling repertoire. Mix and match your plant choices to include different shapes, textures and tones – you'll be surprised how easy it is to create something eye-catching. If your fireplace isn't being used, turn the hearth into an extra plant nook.

Mistletoe cactus, heartleaf philodendron and prayer plant

'GREEN SHELFIES'

They may take a little practice to perfect, but 'green shelfies' are
worth their weight in gold when you get them right. It's not just about
cramming lots of plants onto the shelf. Focus on using spacing,
texture and shape to best effect. Allow tendrils to float downwards
to grab your attention, then create a visual journey that bounces
from one glorious green scene to the next. Pepper the shelves with
personal items in a variety of colours and shapes. It pays to keep
things balanced – if all the plants are on one side, it will look
disjointed. Use a mix of upright and trailing plants to give your
'green shelfie' variation and texture.

An assortment of plants including zanzibar gem, hoya varieties, chain of hearts and leatherleaf fern

EXPERT TIP

A lush hanging plant adds a sense of relaxed elegance, while a well-shaped plant placed alongside interesting artworks adds an extra layer of visual interest. Amplify the effect by adding a mirror.

Heather Nette King, interior stylist and writer

Basil, rosemary and parsley

WINDOWSILLS

Bright, light windowsills are an obvious choice for displaying your plant collection. Whether they're tiny and thin and only fit for small plants, or broad and deep, make the most of what you have. Your plants will thank you for it. Just make sure they're not in constant direct sunlight, especially during the hot summer months.

If you're lucky enough to have a kitchen windowsill, put some hard-working herbs to the test. Basil, rosemary and parsley are easy to care for. They enjoy being plucked for use, and they are the key ingredients of many delicious meals. They also have a beautiful aroma, which is extra helpful when cooking smells are an issue.

Hoya heuschkeliana, krimson queen hoya and fiddle leaf fig

Devil's ivy, mistletoe cactus, Japanese maple and aluminium plant

DARK CORNERS

Most houses have at least one dark corner and that is often exactly where you need to style with plants. There are some plants that can tolerate a dark position, but all plants do need some light to grow. If your dark corner gets a little light, try spath sensation, rubber plant, devil's ivy, zanzibar gem or snake plant. Be sure to keep a watchful eye over them to pick up any light-related issues before they become irreparably damaged. As an option, you could rotate them into a brighter position every other day.

Another option in dark corners is to use cut foliage instead of plants. You still get the overall effect of greenery, but it's a short-term fix which is handy if you're dressing the house for guests for instance.

A trailing chain of hearts

MEZZANINES

Mezzanines can be great for storage, but sometimes they simply turn into dead space. Make the most of a mezzanine by setting up a nook that can be used as a tranquil green refuge. If the adults of the family don't end up using it, the kids will!

07

—

Caring for plants

There are many sources that claim to know how to best care for plants, but the reality is that every indoor environment is different. No-one knows your home as well as you do, and general plant care guidance should be taken with a pinch of salt. You and your neighbour may both have north-facing windows, but your rooms may differ in their humidity, the temperature or how draughty they are. These can all affect a plant's growth. Do some research on your plant's needs, follow those instructions as best you can in your home, and observe them. They'll soon tell you if they're happy or not.

ESSENTIAL TOOLS

There are some beautiful designer plant care tools on the market these days, which look great and do a great job, but high-end pieces aren't necessary. The essentials are a watering can (or any type of watering vessel), a mister or spray bottle and scissors or snips (strong snips can usually do the basic jobs an indoor gardener has to tackle). If you have cacti, get a pair of thick gloves too.

UNDERSTANDING A PLANT'S NEEDS

Plants are complex organisms with essential needs: air, light, water, mineral food materials (or fertiliser), a suitable temperature range and, in most cases, soil to put down roots. Each individual plant has its own requirements, but successful plant care is something that comes with practice (and a little research).

It's important to understand their growth and rest cycle. Most houseplants have an active growth period between spring and autumn, followed by a winter rest period. These cycles can dramatically affect the amount of water you give your plants, and your overall success. Many plants have died at the hand of too much or too little water.

Temperature is a key factor in the successful care of plants. The majority of indoor plants come from tropical or subtropical areas and prefer warmer conditions. Plants do not like extreme changes in temperature, for example, during the hot summer months when we blast the air-conditioning or turn fans on. Move the plants, or position the fans so that the cool air isn't blowing directly on them.

BE ATTENTIVE

The key to keeping plants alive and thriving is to pay attention to
them. Check in on your plants every couple of days and be aware
of what's happening. Are there signs of new growth? Do they look
distressed? How damp or dry is the soil? Are there any bugs on them?

   These regular checks allow you to identify any potential issues
and act quickly, before your plant is damaged beyond repair.

WATERING TIPS

When it's time for watering, it's often easiest to put all your plants in the sink – or bath or shower cubicle, depending on the size of your collection. This way you can give them a good soaking, if required. (Remember that some plants prefer less water, so check their needs first.) Make sure to let the plants drip out before moving them. This ensures your plants get the water they need, and also reduces the risk of any water damage to your floors or furniture. Potted plants with drip trays may not need to be moved.

Before you go away for more than a few days, move your plastic-potted plants to the bath and place them on a moist capillary mat or saucers of damp pebbles. Ensure the plants aren't sitting directly in water, but can draw up moisture as they need it. For plants in ceramic pots, give them a good watering, let them drain and then immediately cover them with plastic bags, securing the bags to the rim of the pot. Use stakes inserted in the soil to keep the bag from touching the plant. You're essentially creating a terrarium-like system. The moisture will remain in the bag for up to three weeks, keeping your plant hydrated while you're gone.

08

—

Plant index

| COMMON NAME | SCIENTIFIC OR LATIN NAME | WATERING | | LIGHT | HUMIDITY |
		GROWTH PERIOD (WARMER MONTHS)	REST PERIOD (COOLER MONTHS)		
African milk tree	*Euphorbia trigona*	◊	◊	⛅ – ☀	∿
African milk tree 'Royal Red'	*Euphorbia trigona* 'Royal Red'	◊	◊	⛅	∿
Agave	*Agave victoriae-reginae*	◊◊◊	◊	⛅ – ☀	∿∿∿
Airplant	*Tillandsia sp.*	◊	◊	⛅	∿∿
Airplant – Spanish moss	*Tillandsia usneoides*	◊	◊	⛅	∿∿
Aloe vera	*Aloe barbadensis* 'Miller'	◊	◊	⛅ – ☀	∿∿
Aluminium plant	*Pilea cadierei*	◊◊◊	◊◊	⛅	∿∿∿
Begonia	*Begonia sp.*	◊◊	◊	⛅	∿∿∿
Bird of paradise	*Strelitzia reginae*	◊◊	◊	☀	∿∿∿
Bird's nest fern	*Asplenium nidus*	◊◊◊	◊◊	⛅	∿∿∿
Boston fern	*Nephrolepis exaltata*	◊◊	◊◊	⛅ – ☀	∿∿ – ∿∿∿
Bunny ear cactus	*Opuntia microdasys*	◊◊	◊	☀	∿
Button Fern	*Pellaea rotundifolia*	◊◊	◊	⛅	∿∿ – ∿∿∿
Cast iron plant	*Aspidistra elatior*	◊◊	◊	☁ – ☁	∿
Century plant	*Agave americana*	◊	◊	☀	∿
Chain of hearts	*Ceropegia woodii*	◊	◊	⛅ – ☀	∿ – ∿∿
Chinese money plant	*Pilea peperomioides*	◊◊	◊	☁ – ⛅	∿∿∿
Christmas cactus	*Schlumbergera truncata*	◊◊◊	◊◊	☁ – ⛅	∿∿
Devil's ivy	*Epipremnum aureum*	◊◊	◊	☁ – ⛅	∿∿ – ∿∿∿
Donkey's tail	*Sedum morganianum*	◊◊	◊	⛅	∿ – ∿∿
Dwarf umbrella tree	*Schefflera arboricola*	◊◊	◊	⛅	∿∿∿ – ∿∿

COMMON NAME	SCIENTIFIC OR LATIN NAME	WATERING		LIGHT	HUMIDITY
		GROWTH PERIOD (WARMER MONTHS)	REST PERIOD (COOLER MONTHS)		
Emerald ripple	*Peperomia caperata*	2 drops	1 drop	part sun/cloud	high waves
Fan aloe	*Aloe plicatilis*	2 drops	1 drop	full sun	low waves
Fiddle leaf fig	*Ficus lyrata*	2 drops	1 drop	part sun/cloud – full sun	high waves – high waves
Fig	*Ficus carica*	2 drops	1 drop	part sun/cloud	low waves – high waves
Firestick plant	*Euphorbia tirucalli*	1 drop	1 drop	full sun	low waves – high waves
Fruit salad plant	*Monstera deliciosa*	2 drops	1 drop	part sun/cloud	high waves
Giant bird of paradise	*Strelitzi nicolai*	2 drops	1 drop	full sun	high waves
Golden cane palm	*Dypsis lutescens*	2 drops	1 drop	part sun/cloud	high waves – high waves
Green exotica hoya	*Hoya carnosa 'Exotica'*	2 drops	1 drop	full sun	high waves
Happy plant	*Dracaena fragrans*	2 drops	1 drop	part sun/cloud	high waves
Heartleaf philodendron	*Philodendron scandens*	2 drops	1 drop	cloud – part sun/cloud	high waves – high waves
Hoya heuschkeliana	*Hoya heuschkeliana*	2 drops	1 drop	full sun	high waves
Hoya odetteae	*Hoya odetteae*	2 drops	1 drop	full sun	high waves
Indian rope hoya	*Hoya carnosa 'Compacta'*	2 drops	1 drop	part sun/cloud – full sun	high waves
Jade	*Crassula ovata*	2 drops	1 drop	full sun	low waves
Japanese aralia	*Fatsia japonica*	3 drops	2 drops	part sun/cloud	high waves
Jitters	*Crassula ovata undulata*	2 drops	1 drop	full sun	low waves
Kentia palm	*Howea forsteriana*	2 drops	1 drop	part sun/cloud	high waves – high waves
Krimson princess hoya	*Hoya carnosa 'Rubra'*	2 drops	1 drop	full sun	high waves
Krimson queen hoya	*Hoya carnosa 'Tricolor'*	2 drops	1 drop	full sun	high waves
Lady palm	*Rhapis excelsa*	2 drops	1 drop	part sun/cloud	low waves – high waves

COMMON NAME	SCIENTIFIC OR LATIN NAME	WATERING		LIGHT	HUMIDITY
		GROWTH PERIOD (WARMER MONTHS)	REST PERIOD (COOLER MONTHS)		
Leatherleaf fern	*Romohra adiantiformis*	💧💧💧	💧💧	partial sun	high
Maidenhair fern	*Adiantum sp.*	💧💧	💧💧	partial sun	high
Mexican snow ball	*Echeveria elegans*	💧	💧	full sun	low
Mini monstera	*Rhaphidophora tetrasperma*	💧💧💧	💧💧	partial sun	high
Mistletoe cactus	*Rhipsalis baccifera*	💧💧💧	💧	shade	high
Mountain Aloe	*Aloe Marlothii*	💧	💧	partial sun – full sun	high
Painted Lady	*Echeveria derenbergii*	💧	💧	full sun	low
Parlour palm	*Chamaedorea elegans*	💧💧	💧	shade – partial sun	low – high
Peace lily	*Spathiphyllum wallisii*	💧💧	💧	shade	high
Peacock plant	*Calathea makoyana*	💧💧💧	💧💧	shade	high
Prayer plant	*Maranta leuconeura*	💧💧💧	💧💧	partial sun	high
Philodendron 'Hope'	*Phildendron selloum x hybrid*	💧💧	💧	partial sun	high
Radiator plant	*Peperomia*	💧	💧	partial sun	high
Royal Hawaiian hoya	*Hoya pubicalyx*	💧💧	💧	full sun	high
Rubber plant	*Ficus elastica*	💧💧	💧	partial sun full sun	low
Satin pothos	*Scindapus pictus 'Argyraeus'*	💧💧	💧	partial sun – full sun	low – high
Snake plant	*Sansevieria trifasciata*	💧💧	💧	shade – full sun	low – medium
Snowdrop cactus	*Rhipsalis houlletiana*	💧💧💧	💧	shade	high
Spath sensation	*Spathiphyllum*	💧💧	💧	shade	high
Spider plant	*Chlorophytum comosum*	💧💧	💧	partial sun – full sun	low – high
Spurge	*Euphorbia sp.*	💧💧	💧💧	partial sun – full sun	low

COMMON NAME	SCIENTIFIC OR LATIN NAME	WATERING		LIGHT	HUMIDITY
		GROWTH PERIOD (WARMER MONTHS)	REST PERIOD (COOLER MONTHS)		
String of pearls	*Senecio rowleyanus*	◊ ◊	◊	⛅ – ☀	〜〜
Umbrella plant	*Schefflera amate*	◊ ◊	◊	⛅	≈ – ≋
Variegated jade vine	*Senecio macroglossus 'Variegatus'*	◊ ◊	◊	⛅ – ☀	〜〜
Variegated monstera	*Monstera borsigiana*	◊ ◊	◊	⛅	≈
Variegated *hoya heuschkeliana*	*Hoya heuschkeliana variegata*	◊ ◊	◊	☀	≈
Weeping fig	*Ficus benjamina*	◊ ◊	◊	⛅	≈
White ghost cactus	*Euphorbia lactea 'White Ghost'*	◊	◊	⛅ – ☀	≈
Zanzibar gem	*Zamioculcas zamiifolia*	◊	◊	☁ – ⛅	≈
Zebra plant	*Aphelandra squarrosa*	◊ ◊	◊	☁ – ⛅	≈ – ≋
Zebra plant (calathea)	*Calathea zebrina*	◊ ◊ ◊	◊ ◊	⛅	≋

INDEX LEGEND		
◊	One Drop	Water sparingly, allowing the mix to nearly dry out between waterings.
◊ ◊	Two Drop	Water moderately, allowing the top 3cm to dry out between waterings.
◊ ◊ ◊	Three Drop	Water generously when surface of mix is dry.
☀	Bright Light	This plant thrives in bright, indirect sunlight and can tolerate periods of direct sunlight.
⛅	Filtered Light	This plant prefers bright filtered sunlight but should not be placed in direct sunlight.
☁	Medium Light	This plant can tolerate shady conditions.
〜〜	Low Humidity	This plant prefers dry atmosphere between 10-40% humidity. Dehumidifiers can be used.
≈	Moderate Humidity	This plant prefers a moderate amount of moisture between 40-60% humidity. Most homes sit at this level, however you can check the humidity with a hyrometer if you are concerned.
≋	High Humidity	This plant prefers a high moisture content with humidity higher than 60%. Mist the leaves of this plant every morning or sit the pot on a pebble tray.

—

Acknowledgements

A heartfelt thanks to everyone involved in this passion project and to our amazing supporters who've brought us this far.

To Paulina and the team at Thames & Hudson, and to our amazing crew: Michelle, Loretta and Ethan, who worked so tirelessly to help us shoot the book. Thank you to our talented contributors: Heather Nette King, Simone Haag, Steve Cordony and Elizabeth Barnett and to our generous prop suppliers.

A massive thank you to the homeowners who so warmly welcomed us into their homes: Karling Hamill (Little Karstar), Dan, Michelle from Bask Interiors, Steve and Lina from St Etienne Daylesford, Jason and Nathan from The Plant Society, Jeremy and Lorelei from The Jacky Winter Group and our amazing friends Raquel and David. We were overwhelmed by your generosity and support.

Special thanks to our collaborator and good friend, photographer Annette O'Brien, for helping bring our vision for *Plant Style* to life. Last, but by no means least, thank you to our friends and families for all their endless support.